Elroy Sparta Trail
Guidebook

Elroy Sparta Trail Guidebook

Also includes: "400" State Trail, Omaha Trail, La Crosse River State Trail, and Great River State Trail

Bob Sobie

Writers Club Press
San Jose New York Lincoln Shanghai

Elroy Sparta Trail Guidebook
**Also includes: "400" State Trail, Omaha Trail, La Crosse River State Trail,
and Great River State Trail**

Writers Club Press
an imprint of iUniverse.com, Inc.

For information address:
iUniverse.com, Inc.
5220 S 16th, Ste. 200
Lincoln, NE 68512
www.iuniverse.com

ISBN: 0-595-18977-6

Printed in the United States of America

I dedicate this book to my family. To Martha who always understands when I *need* to go biking, who proof read this book many times, and whom I love with all my heart. To Carl and Roger who are always willing to go biking with me.

I also dedicate this book to the "Friday Riders:" Alan, Rob, Tom, Tom, and Pete. You guys are the best!

Contents

Preface

A supplement website to this book is available at www.ElroySparta.com. At this website I will provide updated information about trail conditions, resources, prices, vendor changes, trail maps, photographs, and corrections to any typographical mistakes. If you have any comments, additions, or corrections to this book that you would like included either in the website or in future editions of this book, contact the author at ElroySparta@aol.com.

Please visit the website for the latest information at: www.ElroySparta.com

Chapter 1

Introduction

My Heaven on earth! I remember sitting in a Sunday school class when I was 11 years old and the teacher said that Heaven would be similar to my favorite place on earth. Therefore, Heaven must be just like the Elroy Sparta Trail.

The Elroy Sparta Trail is the backbone of 110.5 miles of biking and/or hiking trails that is principally void of motor vehicle traffic. Thus, in my humble opinion, it is the most enjoyable type of recreation there is. Combined with the "400", Omaha, La Crosse River, and Great River Trails, the Elroy Sparta Trail runs through some of the most scenic land in all of the Midwest. This, plus some of the friendliest people you will ever hope to meet, makes this area truly a Heaven for anyone who rides a bicycle.

Elroy Sparta Trail

I have been visiting this trail since 1983, making between one and five trips each and every year. Most of these trips were made with my family, some with good friends, some with my students, and even some solo journeys. I once rode the Elroy Sparta Trail as part of a bachelor party (does this give you a clue as to what I define as excitement). All were better than the previous! Travel to the Elroy Sparta Trail has truly become a pilgrimage for me.

The Elroy Sparta Trail is located in West Central Wisconsin, an area referred to as unglaciated, leaving behind rolling hills and valleys that make this visually stand out from most of the Midwest which was scoured flat by the glaciers many million years ago. Juneau and Monroe Counties lie on the western edge of the Central Wisconsin River plain and in the middle of a recreational wonderland.

The Elroy Sparta Trail is easily accessed by virtue of its close proximity to Interstates 90 and 94. Sparta is located at the intersection of Interstate

90 and Highway 27 (exit 25). Reach Elroy by exiting Interstate 90/94 at the town of Mauston (exit 69), take Highway 82 west to Highway 80, and then travel south on Highways 82 & 80 into downtown Elroy. Highway 71 parallels and crosses the trail at several points making travel between the towns on the trail simple.

The 32-mile Elroy Sparta Trail is enjoyed by many thousands of bicyclists, hikers, cross country skiers, and snowmobilers each year. I have met people from all over the U.S. as well as some from overseas while enjoying this beautiful trail. Many families, like mine, plan their family vacations or weekend getaways with a stop at the trail in mind. Youth organizations such as scouts and school groups find this the perfect location for a fun and safe outing.

Plenty of hotel, motel, bed and breakfast, and camping facilities are in the area, but I would suggest making reservations in advance. During the upcoming chapters I will suggest accommodations, restaurants, and attractions. As you can imagine, weekends can be very crowded while on weekdays you can have the trail to yourself. Small towns, restaurants, antique stores, and friendly people will make your visit complete.

The trail itself is surfaced with limestone screening which makes the surface softer than concrete but hard enough to ride with almost any type of bicycle. I ride a mountain bike when I visit the trail but I have been very successful with skinny road bike tires back before mountain bikes became so popular. I would not suggest that extremely expensive bicycles be used on this trail because of the limestone dust. Children with training wheels and adults pulling children in buggies are often observed. Because the Elroy Sparta Trail is built on an abandoned railroad bed, the trail is virtually flat, no more than a 3% grade. But, be aware that a 3% uphill grade that stretches over a few miles on a semi-soft surface can be a challenge to some younger children or inexperienced riders. The many bridges you will encounter on the trail are covered with wood planks and protected with railings.

The most breath-taking feature of this trail is the tunnels. Three tunnels were cut through the bedrock and range from ¼ mile to ¾ mile long.

Each of the tunnels has its own personality. It gets so dark, damp, and cold in the tunnels that I suggest you bring a jacket and a light. Bicycles must always be walked through the tunnels because you can get very disoriented due to the darkness, crown of the trail, and the strange echoes. This is definitely not the place to be if you are claustrophobic. I always suggest that every child and adult wear an approved bicycle helmet!

For those who would like to bike one direction only, a great shuttle service is available. Out Spokin' Adventures (1-800-4we-bike & www.out-spokinadventures.com) are some of the nicest people I have ever met. They will provide one-way transportation in their van for you and your bicycle for a very reasonable price, and at the same time they will provide you with the history of the trail and suggestions for overnight accommodations and culinary delights. I suggest you meet Out Spokin' Adventures at the Sparta Trailhead parking area and have them drive you to Elroy. With Elroy's elevation of 997 feet and Sparta's elevation of 800 feet you will be spending more time downhill if you travel west. Make sure they drop you off at the Elroy Commons, not the Elroy Parking area, so you can see the commons and the downtown area.

Be aware that weather conditions can change in a moment's notice. I once entered the west end of Tunnel #3 with the sky a truly beautiful light blue and the sun shining brightly. By the time I walked through the tunnel to the east end, I was stopped by a Department of Natural Resources Officer because of a passing funnel cloud and hailstorm. The ride back to the campground that day provided a soaking rain. Once I had to cancel a scheduled bike ride during the second week of May because the snow was too deep. I suggest you prepare for most any type of weather.

During the winter months, the tunnel doors are closed to prevent icing conditions from deteriorating the stones within. If you enjoy snowmobiling be aware that local snowmobile clubs provide marked trails so you can detour the tunnels. Cross-country skiers also need to be aware that the tunnels are not accessible during the winter months.

If your goal is to hike, please be aware that most trail users are bicyclists. Keep alert, especially from behind because bikes can sneak up on you without notice. Most rollerbladers find the surface too soft for good traveling.

No matter what sport you participate in, I would suggest the following safety guidelines. Always carry water, towns can feel like many miles away, especially on a hot day in the sun. Ride or walk single file so that you are not a hazard to people coming around the bend at speed. Keep children within eyesight at all times and teach them to stay on the right side of the trail. When passing another person(s) do so on the left, but only after warning them by saying loudly "on your left." A bright light is a must when in the tunnel; it can become very dark and disorienting. I always carry a cell phone, turned off so as not to disturb a beautiful day, but to use in case of emergencies. Last, but not least, carry a good map. I never leave home without one. Free maps (printed at the back of this book) are available in all of the towns along the trail, but you get what you pay for. My favorite map of the trail comes from American Bike Trails (1430 Main Street, Suite 525, Des Plaines, IL 60016) and is available in better bike stores.

Most importantly, enjoy yourself and the trail. Many thousands travel to the trail every year and return back the next year because they too enjoy themselves. I hope this book will make your visit to the Elroy Sparta Trail more enjoyable.

Chapter 2

History of the Elroy Sparta Trail

In the mid 1800's the railroad tycoons realized that a rail line was needed to bring goods from North and South Dakota through St. Paul, Minnesota to the markets in Chicago, Illinois. Some sections of this rail line were already built, but the section from Winona Junction, Minnesota to Elroy, Wisconsin remained vacant. The La Crosse, Trempealeau, and Prescott Railway Company initially planned the construction of just such a rail line, but lacked the resources to build it. The Chicago and NorthWestern Railroad purchased this company with the direct aim of building the needed rail line.

The Chicago and NorthWestern Railroad completed the railroad bed between Winona Junction and Elroy and officially opened it on September 14, 1873. The first train carrying a distinguished list of local businessmen made the trip on September 15. The rail line was open for normal traffic on September 25, 1873. The feat of opening the rail line was amazing considering all the obstacles the workers encountered. The winter of 1872-73 was extreme with sub-zero temperatures and a deeper than average snowfall. Spring brought torrential rainfalls. The country was in a period of a financial downturn in 1873. Albert Keep, the President of the Chicago and NorthWestern Railroad, was seen as a visionary when he decided to continue construction of the line.

Even considering the economy and the weather conditions, the biggest obstacle to construction of the rail line between the cities of Elroy and Sparta was the hills. To accomplish the task of building a railroad, whose engines could not negotiate steep uphill grades, the railroad decided to tunnel three times through the hillsides. Both Tunnel #1, located between the Villages of Kendall and Wilton, and Tunnel #2, located between the Villages of Wilton and Norwalk, took 1 ½ to 2 years to construct. Both tunnels are 1,680 feet in length. Construction took place by digging and boring from both ends at the same time. Tunnels #1 & #2 had to have their entrances covered with stone blocks to give them strength, but the entire length of tunnel #2 required blocks to be installed because the earth was not strong enough to support the weight of the land above it. Tunnel #2 is the narrowest of the three tunnels so indentations along the sides were included during construction to allow for the switchmen to stand in if they were caught in the tunnel as a train was coming through.

Tunnel #3, completed in 1873, is located between the Village of Norwalk and the City of Sparta and was by far the toughest to build. Because of its length, 3,810 feet, and due to the type and depth of the rock that had to be removed, this tunnel took 3 years and over one million dollars to complete. Construction of this tunnel took place by digging and boring from both ends at the same time as well as boring from the top of the hill downward, to the help remove material. One thousand feet in from the east end of the tunnel, a vertical hole was made from the top of the hill to the tunnel; sixteen hundred feet from the west end of the tunnel, another vertical hole was made from the top of the hill to the tunnel. These holes were used to lift up material and remove it from the tunnel, and these vertical holes were filled in when the construction of the tunnel was completed. Inside the tunnel there is a constant stream of water from a natural spring located approximately at the midpoint. A stone flume, a water diversion ditch, had to be included in the construction for Tunnel #3. This stone flume stretches from the top of the hill that the tunnel passes through to the valley to the east of the tunnel in an effort to divert water that could erode the rail bed and collapse the banks of the valley leading to the tunnel. There is evidence that the stone flume was built after the tunnel as a result of several cave-ins. The stone flume is unfortunately missed by many that don't pay attention to their surroundings as they bike the trail. While visiting the summit area just east of Tunnel #3, walk a few steps north and west across the path and onto the footbridge crossing the flume. Look west for the best view of this massive structure.

At the entrance to each tunnel are massive wood and steel doors. These doors were opened as trains approached the tunnels and then closed after each train passed during the winter months to prevent the moisture inside the tunnels from freezing. Icicles often formed at the entrances near these doors. The railway workers had to constantly attend to these icicles to prevent them from jamming the doors. The door watchmen harbored inside small wooden buildings alongside each of the entrances when not attending to the doors. By wire they kept in contact with nearby stations so they knew when the trains were due at their location. These doors are still closed each winter.

Watchman's Shack

Once in operation, the Elroy to Sparta rail line soon became the main route from western Wisconsin to the western states. Between 1873 and 1911 rail traffic consisted of 6 daily passenger trains and 40 to 50 daily freight trains. The freight trains contained many cars of livestock being sent to the Chicago stockyards. A new rail line was opened in 1911 between Sparta and Olyman Junction then east to the switching yard in West Allis, Wisconsin. This removed through freight trains off the Elroy Sparta section but many local freight trains continued. From 1911 to 1925 a local round trip freight train was added between the towns of Elroy and Sparta only. In 1925, passenger train traffic was reduced to four trains per day. The passenger service was reduced in 1948 to two per day, and in 1953 all passenger train operation was discontinued. Only local freight trains remained on these tracks after 1953. From 1942 to 1947, the Chicago and NorthWestern Railroad routed the famous Mankato 400 passenger train over this line. The "400" was one of the first diesel trains and was know for its speed of delivering passengers from Mankato, Minnesota to Chicago, Illinois in 400 minutes.

Train capacity on the Elroy Sparta line was limited to 600 tons with extra "pusher" engines added to the trains to help with the inclines in the western Wisconsin sections, especially west of Kendall. Just east of the depot in Kendall you may visit the remnants of the 14-stall roundhouse where the extra "pusher" engines were removed from eastbound trains because they would not be needed for the relatively flat pull between Kendall and Chicago. The roundhouse served as a division maintenance shop for the railroad until 1911.

From its opening in 1873 until 1928, the rail bed was maintained by 7 section crews, each crew patrolled and maintained 5 miles of track. In the winter each crew consisted of a foreman and two helpers. During the summer the crews increased by two helpers. In 1928 section crews were reduced to 4, and in 1932 there was another reduction to a total of 3. After the line was abandoned, one crew remained to prevent the rail bed from deterioration. From 1873 until 1912 the section crews traveled the line with handcars. In 1913 the section foreman bought the first motor cars for $43.00 each. The tunnel operators used velocipedes, which were 3 wheeled hand pump vehicles to travel the length of the tunnels.

When the railroad was first built, 60-65 pound rails (determined by the weight for a 3 foot length) were installed. Because of the severe winter snows and icing and the inclines approaching the tunnels, sand was dropped on the rails to provide traction. This deteriorated the rails quickly causing a need for replacement. By 1915, one-half of the rails weighed 72 pounds each and the other half weighed 90-pound each. By 1955, one-half of the rails weighed 100 pounds each while the other half weighed 90 pounds each. Because of moisture in the tunnels, the maintenance here was needed more frequently. The rails in Tunnels #1 & #2 were changed three times while the Tunnel #3 rails were changed a total of four times. In 1949, a 112-pound continuously welded rail was laid in Tunnel #3. The ties in Tunnel #1 were replaced in 1927, and the Tunnel #2 ties were replaced in 1926. All of the ties in Tunnel #3 were changed in 1922 and another 100 ties were changed in 1949. Because of the backbreaking work and cold damp working conditions, the average man could only change three ties each day. In 1949, all of the old ballast rocks were stripped by hand, and 24 carloads of new rock ballast were installed on the rail bed. The crews worked from 4:00 p.m. to midnight to not disrupt the majority of the rail traffic.

Each town along the rail line had its own depot. The depot in Sparta is used today as the Chamber of Commerce headquarters and as a visitor center. Norwalk's depot was built in 1873 but has been severely altered since. The Wilton depot was built in 1873 with 2 waiting rooms added at a later date. Unfortunately, this depot was dismantled in 1968. The Kendall depot was the newest, built in 1900. It contained two waiting rooms. This depot serves as a museum and visitors center today. In the early days, each depot had an agent and 2 operators, with the depot at Norwalk employing one additional agent's helper. The operators each worked a 12-hour day.

Because the railroad installed only one main rail between the cities of Elroy and Sparta, they needed to install several sidetracks so trains could wait for other trains passing in the opposite direction. At one of these side-tracks located between Allen's Crossing and Hickory Hill Crossing (these areas are no longer around), a boxcar was used for a telegrapher's office. Likewise a telegrapher was located on a sidetrack near Tunnel #1. These men would keep track of the location and direction of trains on the line.

On October 15, 1902 near the town of Norwalk, a train traveling on the main line collided with a train that was leaving a sidetrack. This caused the only major train vs. train accident recorded on the line. During a heavy rain in 1908 a large section of the railroad bed was washed away near the town of Wilton causing extensive damage. Photographs of the wash out can be viewed in the depot located in Kendall. Periodically, heavy rains caused mudslides that would disrupt rail traffic. Many other incidents occurred, but all were classified as minor derailments.

The only dignitary that is said to have traveled the rails between Elroy and Sparta is President Harry S. Truman. In 1948 during the campaign for his second term as President of the United States, President Truman's train traveled west through Elroy, Kendall, Wilton, and Norwalk prior to a whistle stop in the City of Sparta.

The Chicago and NorthWestern Railroad ceased all operations on the line between Elroy and Sparta in July 1964. The tracks were removed in 1965. The Wisconsin Conservation Department (now called the Department of Natural Resources or DNR) took ownership of the 660 acre, 32-mile long property on March 3, 1966 for a cost of $12,000.

In a letter to the Chicago Tribune on September 25, 1963, May Theilgaard Watts writes, "We are human beings. We are able to walk on two feet. We need a footpath." At the time of this letter, Ms. Watts was referring to the abandoned Chicago, Aurora, and Elgin Railroad west of Chicago, now called the Illinois Prairie Path. This letter is credited as the birth of the rails-to-trails movement in the United States. She continued to write, "If we have courage and foresight…we can create this strip (as) a proud resource." With this letter began the conversion of the Chicago, Aurora, and Elgin Railroad into the Illinois Prairie Path. Within a few years, the people of Wisconsin started work on converting the Elroy Sparta section of rails into the trail it is today. It is hotly debated which rail-to-trail project was first. It seems that the planning and approval for the Illinois Prairie Path occurred first, but the Elroy Sparta Trail had its grand opening first.

In 1974 the Elroy Sparta National Trails, Incorporated was formed at the request of the DNR. Its purpose is to conduct the business of running the concessions, advertising, promotions, answering questions, as well as other facets of making the Elroy Sparta Trail the haven that it is today. An agree-ment between the Elroy Sparta National Trails, Inc. and the DNR in 1977 gave exclusive rights to concessions on the trail to Elroy Sparta National Trails, Inc. At this same time, the DNR was completing renovations at the Kendall Depot, which became the headquarters of the corporation. The

Elroy Sparta National Trails, Inc. is composed of two representatives from each town on the trail. These directors are sent from the Lions Clubs of each town except the representatives from Sparta are sent from the Jaycees organization. The Elroy Sparta National Trails, Inc. is set up as a not-for-profit non-stock corporation whereby all profits have been reverted to improvements in the facilities.

This type of local enthusiasm is what makes the trail the best Rails-To-Trails project in the country. It is estimated that more than 60,000 people enjoy the trail each year bringing with them the base for a strong tourism guided economy.

I would like to thank the dozens of local residents who have stopped to chat with me about the history of the Elroy Sparta Bike Trail. I would especially like to thank the authors of the following pamphlets, without which I would not have been able to compile this history:

The Blend of Yesterday and Today on the Elroy-Sparta Trail, Department of Natural Resources, Wisconsin.

Anderson, Leonard R., *History of the Chicago-and North Western Railroad Line—Elroy to Sparta—Now Elroy Sparta Trail.*

History of the Elroy Sparta Trail.

Chapter 3

City of Elroy:
Where the Trails Meet

The eastern most end of the Elroy Sparta Trail is the City of Elroy, Wisconsin, population 1,533. Situated just 12 miles west of exit 69 on Interstate 90/94, this town boasts being the center of three trails. The "400" State Trail heads south of Elroy for 22 miles to the City of Reedsburg. The Omaha Trail travels north of Elroy 12.5 miles to the Village of Camp Douglas. The most famous, the Elroy Sparta Trail, heads west of Elroy for 32 miles to the City of Sparta.

In the middle of the Elroy business district you will find the Elroy Commons area in which you will discover many services that the typical trail user needs. Built in 1991, the Commons provides parking, restrooms, showers, bike rentals, child buggy rentals, the best gift shop on the trail, pay phones, area information, picnic tables, and a park that includes a tot lot. This Commons area is a must see for everyone who enjoys the trail.

Across the street from the Commons is Jim's Trailside Deli & Ice Cream Parlor. In this establishment, that has both indoor and outdoor seating, you will find every bike riders favorite, great ice cream. I suggest you try their chocolate malts. Country Favorites is a store that offers a unique mixture of Amish furniture, quilts, figurines, stuffed animals, pottery, and much more. Nelson's NAPA Auto Parts store may be a weekend saver in the case of a breakdown in this area. If you crave fast food, the Elroy Subway Restaurant is just a short walk from the Commons on Highway 80. Nearby, you will find a full service bank, Hansen's IGA grocery store, gas station, restaurants, as well as many other small shops. Stop by the Historical Society Museum and the Carnegie Library to fully understand the flavor of this area.

The west fork of the Baraboo River offers the angler both trout and pan fishing. Schultz City Park on the southern edge of town has facilities for camping (I never stayed here) including RV electrical hookups, a swimming pool, and showers for their camping guests. Just 1 mile from the Commons on the Elroy Sparta Trail is the Allan Thompson walk-in only camping area managed by the Department of Natural Resources. This camping area is one of the favorites by those who like to rough it. Here you will find pit toilets, picnic tables, and grassy sites. It is amazingly quiet considering how close to town it is. Parking is available nearby alongside the trail. Be careful, you will have to hike up a very steep hill to access the camping area. All camping sites are on a first come first serve basis. This campground is unmanned, just fill out the registration form and place your campground fee in the box provided.

One of the most famous residents of the City of Elroy is Tommy Thompson, long time former Governor of Wisconsin and currently the Secretary of Health and Human Services in the Cabinet of President George W. Bush. I understand that Secretary Thompson hasn't spent much time in his hometown since becoming Governor, so don't plan on running in to him while cycling on the trail.

The only negative experience I have ever had while visiting the Elroy Sparta Trail happened in the City of Elroy. The Chief of Police pulled me over for driving 4 miles per hour over the speed limit. I was only driving 29 miles per hour! Be careful to watch your speed while passing through this area.

If there was one thing that the City of Elroy could do to make a tremendous improvement for visitors, it would be to attract a motel chain to build near the trail. Right now you have to travel 12 miles to the City of Mauston to stay in a motel that appears familiar. However, if you like small hometown charm, Elroy is a great town to visit.

━━━━━

To get to the City of Elroy, Wisconsin, take Interstate 90/94 to the Mauston exit # 69. Proceed on Highway 82 (Highway 82 makes many turns in Mauston) west 11 miles to Highway 80. Highway 82 west and Highway 80 south merge at this point.

To get to the Elroy Commons, take Highway 82 west and Highway 80 south (once they merge) for 1.2 miles to Cedar Street. Turn left on Cedar Street for .2 mile to a stop sign at Second Street (not marked). Turn right on Second Street and proceed for .1 mile. Turn right on Juneau Street, and take this street one block to the Elroy Commons. For those who travel with a GPS, the coordinates of the Elroy Commons are N 43 44.394—W 90 16.217 with an elevation of 997 feet.

To get to the Elroy Trailhead parking, take Highway 82 west and Highway 80 south (once they merge) for 1.2 miles to Highway 71. Turn right on Highway 71 west for .4 mile. The Elroy Trailhead is on the right. For those who travel with a GPS, the coordinates of the Elroy Trailhead parking area are N 43 44.819—W 90 16.776 with an elevation of 918 feet.

In case of emergencies the Elroy Police Department and ambulance respond to 911.

For information contact the Elroy Area Advancement Corporation, 1-800-606-bike, P.O. Box 52, Elroy, WI 53929. The town's web site is www.elroywi.com and email is elroywi@mwt.net.

Chapter 4

Elroy to Kendall:
Wetland and Animal Watching

I have actually overheard people say that this section of the trail is boring. Boy are they wrong! The section of the Elroy Sparta Trail between the City of Elroy and the Village of Kendall is the flattest and straightest section of trail, it does not contain a tunnel, and it follows a fairly busy two-lane state road. But, what this great section has to offer is spectacular wetlands with abundant wild life. It is the only true wetland along the trail because it is the headwater of the Baraboo River system. I suggest that you ride this section slowly while keeping your eyes searching both near and far.

Muskrats, skunks, ground hogs, snakes, raccoons, beavers, songbirds, birds of prey, and a rumored bald eagle or two are just a few of the animals and birds that you may encounter along the way depending on the time of year. Because the majority of this section of the trail is open to the wetlands and farms, spotting the occasional owl or a far off deer is very easy. I suggest you carry a pair of binoculars for the best viewing.

The trail crosses over the Baraboo River (maybe more of a stream at this point) 10 different times in the span of 6 miles. Each river bridge is built on the original rail span with proper modifications to allow both foot and bicycle traffic. Stop along the way to appreciate the construction remembering that these bridges were built in the late 1800's. If you walk down to the river, you may observe many species of small fish and enjoy the call of a bullfrog.

About halfway between Elroy and Kendall, the first of the grand sandstone ledges will greet you on the left. This particular stone grouping is striking because of the water from the river running at its base and wildlife that often feed in the area while perched on rocks. The vegetation here includes many species of prairie grasses, trees, and moss covered rocks. This is one of my favorite places to stop and enjoy life in the slow lane. Just ahead, you will enjoy stone ledges on the right. These ledges rise straight up forming a sheer wall providing the perfect shade for many of Mother Nature's small creatures.

The area just before milepost 5 used to be the biggest eyesore on the trail until the people of the area rectified the situation. An old car graveyard borders the trail and made the trail look dreadful. A large privacy wall painted to blend in with the surroundings now covers the area, and vegetation is gradually taking over to provide a natural barrier. Thank you!

On the approach to the Village of Kendall you will see a private campground on the right, many buildings to the left including a church and a motel, and the remnants of the railroad roundhouse on the right (described in the next chapter).

The Elroy Sparta Trail between the City of Elroy and Village of Kendall is 6 miles long.

This section of the trail may be bicycled in either direction, but be aware that a drop of 91 feet in elevation will make riding eastbound slightly easier.

Parking, food, bicycle rental, concessions, and restrooms are available in the City of Elroy at the Commons, and parking and restrooms are available at the Elroy Trailhead area.

Parking, food, bicycle rental, concessions, and restrooms are available in the Village of Kendall at the depot. Be sure to stop at the Kendall Depot and delight in the museum, do not ride past this treasure.

Chapter 5

Village of Kendall:
Home of the Depot

While biking west on the Elroy Sparta Trail, you are welcomed into the Village of Kendall (population 350) by two very different sites, a small local church and the reminders of past wars. Adjacent to the trail and just east of downtown is a wonderful local church that invites you to service every Sunday. If you time it just right you can hear the church members of St. John's Lutheran Church proudly singing as you pedal by on Sunday mornings. Just across Highway 71 you will find Glenwood Park which displays military aircraft and tanks from past wars. You will find this park full of children playing baseball during the summer months and plenty of playground equipment just begging to be used. Washrooms, drinking water, and plenty of parking are also available here.

Immediately east of town (just west of the Baraboo River) along the north side of the trail lie the remnants of the railroad roundhouse. The roundhouse was used to perform maintenance on the passing trains, but its most important role was to store the pusher engines. West of Kendall was considered the hill section, which required that an extra engine be installed on the heavy freight trains to help them navigate up inclines. East of Kendall was relatively flat all the way to Chicago, so the pusher engine could be removed on all eastbound freight trains. I recommend you take a few minutes to stretch your legs and walk around this monument to the railroads of the past.

The Kendall Depot is on the trail in downtown Kendall. Built in 1900 and restored in 1977, it is the newest of the depots on the trail. In the early days, this depot had an agent and 2 operators who each worked a 12-hour day. The two waiting rooms are now filled with period pieces and an extensive photo collection of what life along the railroad was like. Inside the depot you will be able to purchase souvenirs of the trail such as shirts, mugs, and whistles. Bicycle rentals and a driver shuttle service is available, but call first. This depot also serves as the trail's information center and has very knowledgeable and helpful people stationed in the old agent's cage. Parking is plentiful including parking places long enough for vehicles towing trailers. If your visit to the area does not include this depot, you will be sorry.

Kendall offers many amenities for the trail user: a gas station, grocery store, pay laundry, bars, and restaurants. If you are hungry, I suggest the Midway Restaurant & Bar. Here you will find family dining that is priced right and tastes fine. Pass through the adjoining wall into one of the better typical Wisconsin bars for a great evening of music and conversation.

The Country Livin' Motel is located on the eastern edge of town and just 20 yards from the trail. This 8-unit motel offers clean affordable rooms with air conditioning, television, playground equipment, and barbecue grills. There are even two rooms with whirlpools to enjoy after a hard day on the bicycle.

———

To get to Kendall, Wisconsin, take Interstate 90/94 to the Mauston exit # 69. Proceed on Highway 82 west 11 miles to Highway 80. Take Highway 82 west and Highway 80 south (once they merge) for 1.2 miles to Highway 71. Turn west on Highway 71 for 6 miles to the center of the Village of Kendall. Turn right on White Street for ½ block to the depot.

For those who travel with a GPS, the coordinates of the Kendall Depot are N 43.47.591—W 90.22.112 with an elevation of 1009 feet.

In case of emergencies in Kendall call 1-608-463-7214 for police, and for ambulance service call 911 or 1-608-463-7110.

For information contact the trail headquarters information center at 1-608-463-7109.

Kendall Food Center, near the depot on Highway 71, 1-608-463-3663

Country Livin' Motel, Highway 71, 1-608-463-7135 or 1-608-463-7329

Midway Restaurant & Bar, Highway 71, Downtown Kendall, 1-608-463-7170

Chapter 6

Kendall to Wilton:
Including Tunnel #1

While in the Village of Kendall be sure to eat some calories to prepare you for the climb out of town. Be very careful crossing Highway 71 as you are leaving downtown. The road crosses at a severe angle, and a curve in the road causes blind spots and the false feeling that vehicles are farther away than you think.

From Highway 71 until Tunnel #1 is the most challenging uphill climb. Be aware that the grade may be only two to three percent, but it lasts almost three miles! My children were able to ride this section without rest by the age of 8, but I usually worry less about children than out of shape adults.

The trail changes flavor from a wetland/farmland east of Kendall to tall dense tree growth west of the village. You will cross the Baraboo River one last time. A few miles further west you will cross over a local dirt road (Eagle Dr.) on an impressively tall bridge.

Pay attention to the ground on both sides of the trail. During construction of the railroad, the grade needed to be leveled to allow the trains the traction and power to pull the heavy loads uphill and the ability to brake to stop heavily burdened trains on the downhill sections. As the terrain's elevation changes, the rail bed needed to either be built up or dug out of the earth to keep the grade constant.

The first sign that you are approaching Tunnel # 1 is that the trail will become a carved out valley in the rock walls. Just a few dozen feet before the east end of the tunnel, a restored brakeman warning structure looms high above the trail. This wooden structure was built for the train brakeman who would ride on top of the train cars. Because the tunnel was designed and built to just fit the largest train car, being on top of the train in the tunnel was something to definitely avoid.

Each of the three tunnels has its own personality, each being constructed differently with the entrances carved into the surrounding rock. I think Tunnel #1 is the most scenic. Fewer stone blocks were needed to strengthen the entrances because the natural rock terrain was able to provide the needed support. The entrances to this tunnel are always a favorite with most people stopping short to take photographs. The internal walls are natural rock carved roughly and unevenly providing the visitor with an impression of the tremendous work involved to create this masterpiece. This tunnel is only 1,680 feet in length and the driest of the three. If you get the chance to drive your vehicle in this area make sure you turn south off of Highway 71 on County Road V and drive over Tunnel #1. You will be impressed by the difference in the terrain from the dense woods alongside the trail to the farming area along the road above the tunnel.

Tunnel #1

Watch for a marker approximately ½ mile west of the tunnel on the right. A signpost indicates the spot where the steam engine powered trains would stop for a water fill and to load and unload some of their goods. A picnic table is located here to provide a great resting spot.

Approximately 1-½ miles west of the tunnel, you will come upon Tunnel Trail Campground. Without a doubt this is the best family campground along the trail. I have camped here more than 25 times, always with a smile on my face. A family run business, this campground rests in a valley surrounded by a dense tree line and affords you with just about anything a camper could need. Campsites range from small grassy tent sites to full size pull through paved slabs with full hook-ups. A camping cabin is available for those who do not own their own equipment. Two large shower/restroom houses and a small store to supply you with the essentials are in the buildings on this property. Forgot your bike? Tunnel Trail Campground would be happy to rent you one. The most popular amenity to be found here is the heated swimming pool. Nothing beats a good swim after a long bike ride. Because of the lay of the land, mosquitoes find this area unfriendly, making this one of the only campgrounds in Wisconsin where insect bites are seldom a problem. For those not staying at the campground, you can still enjoy a cold drink or an ice cream treat in the camp store. Be sure to stop by the office and say hello to Julie for me.

Getting hungry, you must stop at the Dorset Valley School Restaurant & Bakery. This restored one room schoolhouse was a school from 1870 until the spring of 1963. It was used for storage until February of 2000 when it became a restaurant. It is located on Highway 71 approximately 2 miles west of Tunnel #1 and is easily accessed by bike. The best restaurant in this area provided with a very nice atmosphere that contains all local Amish built furniture makes this stop a must see. Many of the food products you can enjoy here were raised on the adjoining farm. When leaving the restaurant ask if you can pull the cord that still operates the old school bell. Around the corner is the Amish Furniture & Gift Shop featuring local craftsmen and their beautifully designed and built tables, chairs, hutches, etc. Trail-Side Bed & Breakfast is also on the same property featuring a pool and deck area for relaxation.

As you continue your trek west on the trail, you will find the trail is primarily downhill except for an incline to cross the bridge over Highway 71. Eight bridges to cross the Kickapoo River and its many tributaries are found between the Highway 71 crossing and the Village of Wilton. Downtown Wilton will greet you with a restored caboose.

The Elroy Sparta Trail between the Villages of Kendall and Wilton is 9 miles long.

This section of the trail may be bicycled either direction, but be aware a drop of 236 feet in elevation will make riding westbound slightly easier.

From Kendall west to Tunnel #1 is a short uphill and from Tunnel #1 to Wilton is a long downhill.

Parking, food, bicycle rental, concessions, and restrooms are available in Kendall at the depot. Be sure to stop at the Kendall depot and relish the museum.

Parking, food, camping, and restrooms are available in Wilton.

Tunnel Trail Campground, 1-608-435-6829 (in season) & 1-920-294-3742 (off-season), Route 1 Box 185, Wilton, WI. 54670. Tunneltrail@elroynet.com

Dorset Valley School Restaurant & Bakery, 1-800-775-0698

Trail-Side Bed & Breakfast, 1-800-775-0698 or 1-608-435-6525

To get to Tunnel Trail Campground, take Interstate 90/94 to the Mauston exit # 69. Proceed on Highway 82 west 11 miles to Highway 80. Take Highway 82 west and Highway 80 south (once they merge) for 1.2 miles to Highway 71. Turn west on Highway 71 for 11 miles to the campground. (Alternate route: Take Interstate 90 to the Tomah exit #41. Proceed on Highway 131 south for 10 miles to Highway 71. Turn east for 1.1 miles.) For those who travel with a GPS, the coordinates of Tunnel Trail Campground are N 43 49.505—W 90 27.174 with an elevation of 1196 feet.

To get to Dorset Valley School Restaurant & Bakery and the Trail-Side Bed & Breakfast, take Interstate 90/94 to the Mauston exit # 69. Proceed on Highway 82 west 11 miles to Highway 80. Take Highway 82 west and Highway 80 south (once they merge) for 1.2 miles to Highway 71. Turn west on Highway 71 for 11.9 miles to the restaurant. (Alternate route: Take Interstate 90 to the Tomah exit #41. Proceed on Highway 131 south for 10 miles to Highway 71. Turn east for .2 mile.) For those who travel with a GPS, the coordinates of Dorset Valley School Restaurant & Bakery are N 43 49.892—W 90 28.120.

Chapter 7

Village of Wilton:
The Heart of the Trail

As you are riding westbound on the Elroy Sparta Trail, the first sign that you are in the Village of Wilton is when you encounter the restored caboose on your left. Immediately north of the trail by the caboose you will find restrooms, water, and plenty of free parking.

This small picturesque village (population 478) is surrounded by hills and is primarily a farming community. With a slogan of "The Heart of the Trail" the people of this town really know how to treat their guests. Visitors are invited to camp at the village park for a fee of $5.00/night for adults and $3.00/night for children under 18. Here you will find washrooms, showers, volleyball courts, baseball diamonds, sites with electrical outlets ($1.00 extra per night), and the village swimming pool ($2.00 per day per person). On Sunday mornings during the summer months, the Wilton Lions Club prepares a pancake breakfast in the village park that can't be beat.

Gina's Pies Are Square is the place to eat. Located just three blocks south of the caboose on Main Street you will enjoy a varied menu including some of the best-baked deserts in this section of earth. Daily specials, coffees, Italian sodas, beer & wine all surrounded by antiques makes Gina's the place to eat in Wilton.

Looking for something on the lighter side to eat or to just restock your water bottle with a sport drink? The Wilton Fastrip along the trail on the west edge of town is the place for you. Situated alongside the trail with a conveniently located picnic table, the Wilton Fastrip is often very busy on a hot summer's day.

I find the perfect companion exercise to bicycling is canoeing. Arguably the best river for the novice and/or family to canoe is the Kickapoo River out of Ontario, Wisconsin (population 407) just a few miles south of the Village of Wilton. Locals call the Kickapoo the "crookediest river on earth." The word Kickapoo comes from an Algonquin word meaning "he who goes here, then there." This river makes so many bends that it is possible for you to paddle three hours and only be a few miles as the bird flies from your starting point. A quiet canoe trip along the Kickapoo will find you paddling alongside large cliffs, farms, and forest areas. You truly get the feeling of being in the wilderness without ever being far from civilization. I recommend that you rent your canoe from the strangely titled but always friendly Titanic Canoe Rental in Ontario, Wisconsin. Titanic has very good equipment (Old Town Discovery Canoes) and friendly advice for paddlers of all skill levels. You put the canoes in the river right next to Titanic's headquarters and paddle down river to a predetermined pick-up point of your choosing where Titanic will meet you for the shuttle back to your car. Of the canoe rental companies I have worked with, Titanic sits near the top!

Also located near the town of Ontario you will find Wildcat Mountain State Park. Camping, hiking trails, and a landing for the Kickapoo River are just some of the things to see in this park that sits atop one of the taller hills in the area. Wildcat Mountain State Park is also the Department of Natural Resources headquarters for the Elroy Sparta Trail.

To get to Wilton, Wisconsin, take Interstate 90 to the Tomah exit #41. Proceed on Highway 131 south 10 miles to Highway 71. Turn west for 3.2 miles to the Village of Wilton. Turn right on County M (Main Street). Proceed .1 mile to the caboose on the left side of the street. For those who travel with a GPS, the coordinates of the Wilton Caboose are N 43 48.996—W 90 31.706 with an elevation of 960 feet.

In case of emergencies in Wilton call 911.

Gina's Pies Are Square, 400 Main Street, Wilton, WI 54670, 1-608-435-6541. For those of you who travel with a GPS, the coordinates of Gina's are N 43 48.793—W 90 31.688.

Wilton Fastrip, Highway 71, Wilton, WI 54670, 1-608-435-6977. For those of you who travel with a GPS, the coordinates of Wilton Fastrip are N 43 48.857—W 90 31.896.

Wilton Village Park information, 1-608-435-6666, www.windingrivers.com/wilton.html. You will find the village park by taking Main Street (where the caboose and the trail meet) south .2 mile, then turn east on Center Street for .1 mile to East Street. Turn right and go .1 mile directly into the park. For those of you who travel with a GPS, the coordinates of the Wilton Village Park are N 43 48.719—W 90 31.528.

To get to Ontario, Wisconsin, take Interstate 90 to the Tomah exit #41. Proceed on Highway 131 south 10 miles to Highway 71. Turn west for 3.4 miles to Highway 131 and turn left. Take Highway 131 south for 7.6 miles.

Titanic Canoe Rental, Highway 131 & Main Street, Ontario, WI 54651, 1-608-337-4551 & 1-877-get-sunk, www.titaniccanoerental.com, jasonteynot@hotmail.com. For those who travel with a GPS, the coordinates of Titanic Canoe Rental are N 43 43.439—W 90 35.292.

Wildcat Mountain State Park, Ontario, WI 54651, 1-608-337-4775

Chapter 8

Wilton to Norwalk:
Including Tunnel #2

West of the Village of Wilton will be an uphill climb for the two miles until Tunnel #2. Along the way you will cross one local road and a stream that is a tributary of the Kickapoo River.

Tunnel #2

If your visit finds you in this area during a wet season, watch for the waterfall on the north side of the trail a few dozen yards east of Tunnel #2. This becomes a small trickle during dry weather, but during the wet season it is an interesting site to see. Tunnel #2 is the same length as Tunnel #1 but with much different construction. Massive stone blocks mark both entrances where the surrounding rock is set back more than in Tunnel #1. The entrances to Tunnel #2 are the most photographed location along the trail because of the stone block construction. Along the north side of the trail and very near the east entrance to Tunnel #2, you will see the remnants of a landside that occurred a few years back during a heavy spring rainstorm. Local authorities and volunteers shoveled the fallen earth and debris then shored up the earth to prevent similar occurrences from happening in the future. Be sure to stop and read the trail signs while at the entrances to Tunnel #2 to learn about the history of this area. Because the earth is softer in this location, stone blocks line the interior for its entire length to support the tunnel. A unique feature of this tunnel is the indentations along the sides to allow the switchmen to take shelter if they were caught in the tunnel as a train approached. Because of humidity and moisture dripping through the stone blocks, this is a wet tunnel. Although some water drips on your head, it mostly runs alongside the trail in two small streams in this tunnel. As you walk through Tunnel #2 it is hard to believe that Highway 71 crosses overhead. Likewise, when driving on Highway 71 you see no signs of the trail beneath you.

The 4-mile ride west of Tunnel #2 to the Village of Norwalk is very pleasant and slightly downhill. Marked by thick woods along both sides of the trail and beautiful hills to look at in the distance, it is a pleasure to bicycle ride on this section of the Elroy Sparta Trail. The trail runs alongside and crosses over Moore Creek. The trail also crosses several small roads before intersecting Highway 71 one more time before the trail ends up in downtown Norwalk.

The Elroy Sparta Trail between the Village of Wilton and the Village of Norwalk is 6 miles long.

This section of the trail may be bicycled either direction, there is only a 39 foot drop in total elevation when traveling eastbound. From Wilton west to Tunnel #2 is a short uphill and from Tunnel #2 to Norwalk is a long downhill.

Parking, food, camping, swimming, and restrooms are available in Wilton.

Parking, food, camping, and restrooms are available in Norwalk.

Chapter 9

Village of Norwalk: Gateway to the Tunnels

As you approach the eastern edge of the Village of Norwalk, it is best to hold your breath if the wind is blowing out of the south. The Valley Pride Meat Packing plant located just off the trail as you cross Highway 71 has caused many a bike rider to test their sprinting skills along this section of the Elroy Sparta Trail. Alongside the trail in downtown Norwalk, you will be delighted to see a wide park and many services that the typical trail user requires. A large parking lot is located just across the street just west of the park and adjacent to the trail.

The Lions Club has been very active building huge shelters in this park with picnic tables beneath to provide visitors with a shady place to rest. Free tent camping north of the trail with washrooms, shelters, picnic tables, and a coin operated shower prove again the friendliness of small town Wisconsin.

Judy's Trail Café is one of the most popular stops along the trail as proven by the long lines on hot weekends. Judy's provides breakfast, lunch, and dinner menus as well as many ice cream treats. Inside sitting is available, but most trail users enjoy the walk-up window service and the many picnic tables in the park. Don't expect quick service at Judy's, but do expect friendly service and good food.

Diamond Lil's is an old fashion saloon just off the trail on Highway 71. Here you can enjoy a cold beer and a burger while watching a game on the television. In the back you can sit outside and enjoy a volleyball game or two.

Norwalk is also known as the Black Squirrel Capital of the World, although I have yet to see a black squirrel in this town. By the way, I have also been to the White Squirrel Capital of the World, which is Olney, Illinois. Norwalk has a population of 564, and it offers its visitors a grocery store, gas station/store, and many churches.

~~~~~~~

To get to Norwalk, Wisconsin, take Interstate 90 to the Sparta exit # 28. Proceed on Highway 16 west 1 mile to Highway 71. Turn east on 71 for 12.3 miles to Norwalk. Where Highway 71 turns right, continue straight on Railroad Street .1 mile to the village park and trail parking lot. For those who travel with a GPS, the coordinates of the Norwalk Park are N 43 49.981—W 90 37.259 with an elevation of 1020 feet.

In case of emergencies in Norwalk dial 911.

For information contact the Norwalk Village Office, P.O. Box 51, Norwalk, WI 54648, 1-608-823-7760, www.windingrivers.com/norwalk.html, villageofnorwalk@centuryinter.net.

Diamond Lil's, 201 Main Street (Highway 71), Norwalk, WI 54648, 1-608-823-7708

Judy's Trail Café, Mill Street & the trail, Norwalk, WI 54648

Chapter 10

Norwalk to Sparta: Including Tunnel #3

At 11 miles, this section is the longest stretch between towns on the Elroy Sparta Trail. On your way west out of the Village of Norwalk, the trail crosses two small creeks that serve as part of the Tri-Creek Watershed Project Reservoir, which was built to prevent flooding in the area. The trail also crosses Summit Rd. (County Road T). Along this section of the trail visitors enjoy a mix of woods, pastures, and large rock outcroppings.

Stone Flume

Approximately 2.75 miles west of Norwalk and .25 miles east of Tunnel #3 you will find the Summit Rest Area. Plan to spend some time exploring this fascinating area. On the south side of the trail sits one of the original watchman's shacks which was moved to this location and restored. Tunnel watchmen were located at the entrances to each of the tunnels, and their job included opening and closing the massive wood and steel doors to the tunnels during the winter months. Inside this small building you will find photographs depicting the life of the railroad workers during the heyday of the railroad. Near the watchman's shack an old fashion water pump provides very cold well water with a slight iron taste that can't be beat. I always dump the city water out of my water bottles and fill up from this pump. You will also find nearby picnic tables, sitting benches, and a pit washroom.

Across the trail and a few steps west sits a stone flume that stretches from the top of the hill that the tunnel passes through to the valley to the east. It was built to divert water that might have eroded the rail bed and collapse the banks of the valley leading to the tunnel. The stone flume is unfortunately missed by many who don't pay attention to their surroundings as they bicycle the trail. It is well worth your time to stand on the bridge that crosses the stone flume and look west for the best view of this massive structure.

Inside Tunnel #3

Tunnel #3 is often the favorite of many visitors, probably because it's the longest (3,810 feet). Additionally, when in the middle of this tunnel it is possible, depending on the weather conditions, to not see either end. Total darkness. This happens when the outdoor weather is humid causing the tunnel entrances to become covered with fog. Construction of this tunnel took place by digging and boring from both ends at the same time as well as boring from the top of the hill downward to help remove material. One thousand feet in from the east end of the tunnel, a vertical hole was made from the top of the hill to the tunnel; sixteen hundred feet from the west end of the tunnel, another vertical hole was made from the top of the hill to the tunnel. These holes were used to lift up material and remove it from the tunnel, and these vertical holes were filled in when the construction of the tunnel was completed. Inside the tunnel there is a constant stream of water from a natural spring located approximately at the midpoint, and the water from this spring finds its way through these drilled holes. Make sure you have on clothes that you don't mind getting wet. No matter when you visit, very cold water will rain on you throughout this tunnel, and in some isolated spots a virtual deluge of icy water may pour over your head. Just plan to get wet. At four locations inside this tunnel you will see recent construction to strengthen the tunnel walls and ceiling. Expect most anything in this tunnel. For example, I led a group of college age students through Tunnel #3 one year when a 24-year-old army reserve officer in my group freaked out because of the close confines. It literally took all the energy I had to talk and partially carry/pull this 200-pound student out of the tunnel. On another occasion, I entered the west end of this tunnel with the sky a beautiful shade of blue, but when I reached the east end of the tunnel a hailstorm and a funnel cloud was passing by. Be sure that you walk through all tunnels, but this is especially true of Tunnel #3. Because of the length, the darkness, the water falling on your head, and the echo of the water running along both sides of the trail, many people become disoriented and often cross the centerline into the path of the people walking the opposite direction. Always bring a light into all tunnels.

Just west (.2 mile) of Tunnel #3 on the south side of the trail, you will find the only private rest area along the trail. A very enterprising local property owner placed a soft drink machine, a couple of picnic tables, and a garbage can for trail users. A very friendly individual, I once saw this property owner chase a group of boy scouts down the trail to return a flashlight one of the scouts left behind on the picnic table. Caution, on hot weekends this rest area can become very busy with people seeking relief from the soft drink machine.

Shortly west of the private rest area the trail passes under Highway 71 via a recently built bridge. Between this point and Sparta, the trail crosses many local roads and the Farmers Valley Creek. Since Fort McCoy Military Reservation is located a few short miles north of this section of the trail, watch for the occasional military aircraft flying low on maneuvers.

While bicycling along this section, notice that the ground surrounding the old rail bed drops off significantly leaving the trail sitting much higher than the surrounding farmland. This is an area where the rail bed was built upon a three-mile long wooden trestle. When the trestle became old and unsafe, dirt was packed underneath the rail bed and around the wooden structure, lending strength and support to the old trestle. Unfortunately there is no trailside markers describing this interesting bit of history. Most people bike ride over this section and do not realize what once was here.

With one mile until the west trailhead parking area, the feel of the trail is ruined by new home construction. At this point the trail looses its charm and feels more like suburbia. I hope the elected officials who control the zoning in this area will quickly put a stop to all new construction that can be seen from the trail before the world loses a true American treasure.

A very large sandstone outcropping marks the beginning of the Department of Natural Resources walk-in campground. Although many visitors feeling the need to carve their names into the stone have marred this sandstone, this is still a natural site to behold. The DNR campground provides close parking, grassy tent sites, pit toilets, fire rings, picnic tables, and drinking water. As an unmanned campground, visitors are asked to fill out the registration forms and drop the form with the campground fees in the box provided near the parking area. Because of this campground's location to the Interstate, it is not quiet. The sound of cars and trucks may keep the light sleepers from the rest they require. Within one-half mile of the large sandstone structure, the trailhead with abundant parking, pit washrooms, and water is hard to miss. For many years this was the Sparta end of the trail. Now you can ride through the parking lot to the local road (Igloo Rd.), turn right, cross Interstate 90, and you will find that the bike trail will soon continue on your left (.6 mile on Igloo Rd.). Follow this approximately one-half mile to the Sparta Depot.

Sandstone Ledge

The Elroy Sparta Trail between the Village of Norwalk and the City of Sparta is 11 miles long.

This section of the trail may be bicycled either direction, but be aware that a drop of 211 feet in elevation will make traveling westbound slightly easier. From Norwalk west to Tunnel #3 is a long uphill, and from Tunnel #3 to Sparta is a longer downhill.

Parking, food, camping, and restrooms are available in Norwalk.

Parking, food, camping, restrooms, and most anything you could need or want is available in Sparta.

Chapter 11

City of Sparta:
Bicycling Capital of America

Of course I have not experienced every town in America, but for me Sparta is correct in calling itself the "Bicycling Capital of America." Located at the west end of the Elroy Sparta Trail and the east end of the La Crosse River State Trail, this town is truly in the middle of all your recreational needs. By far the largest city along the trail with a population of 7,788, you will be able to find just about anything that you could need in this area. With a large vibrant downtown business district and many more businesses along the highway, Sparta should be on the list of stops for every trail user.

Worlds' Largest Bicycle

The City of Sparta enjoys doing everything large. It boosts the world's largest bicycle, which is located on the corner of Wisconsin Street and Water Street. A must see when in the area.

Golf, swimming, downhill/cross-country skiing, hunting, snowmobiling, canoeing, kayaking, and of course bicycling are just a few of the sports that may be enjoyed in Sparta. The Monroe County Local History Museum & Research Room is free of charge and a good place to gain an appreciation of the area. The Deke Slayton Memorial Space & Bike Museum (NASA Astronaut Deke Slayton was born nearby) is worth the $2.50 for adults and $1.00 for children ages 6-12 and is an interesting stop for people of all ages. I especially enjoy the large selection of antique bicycles on display.

The original train depot serves as both a visitors center and the Chamber of Commerce Headquarters. Inside, a concession stand offers many opportunities to purchase memorabilia of your visit.

Sparta Depot

Though there are many fine places to eat in the City of Sparta, you will find no better place than Len and Barb's Slice of Chicago. Without a doubt this restaurant is the premier place to eat. Being from the Chicago area, I am always hesitant when I see a restaurant that claims to have Chicago style food, but this place does it right. They may be known for their pizza (which is excellent), but I suggest the Lasagna and my wife suggests the Sparta Turnover. You enter onto the front porch of this old house, now used as the waiting room, then into the living room, currently the restaurant, where you will see only 6 tables. Len will greet you with a picture matching game that I can't seem to ever beat and an offer of a drink while you wait for your meal to arrive.

Another must for the bicycle rider is the A&W drive-in. A true to life drive-in with carhops that deliver the rootbeer floats to your car window. By now it must seem that I spend a fair amount of time eating, you're right.

There are many fine motels in the City of Sparta, but my favorite is the Country Inn. The free continental breakfast is great. The rooms are comfortable, although maybe on the small side. The motel is located just off the interstate exchange and only a few blocks on local roads from the trail. Nothing feels as good as their indoor hot tub and swimming pool after a long day of bicycling.

If you are looking for a more economical place to bed down, you have many choices. The Heritage Motel provides a clean room and bed but not much more. However, you can't beat the price. Leon Valley Campground, just south of town, is a nice family campground that offers 100 sites, cabins, a pool, water & electric sites, and seasonal rates. The Wisconsin Department of Natural Resources provides a walk-in only primitive camp area at the Sparta Trailhead parking area. This is first come first serve and does not offer much more than pit toilets and drinking water.

When the day comes for me to retire from the rat race in the Chicago suburbs, I can't imagine another place I would rather live than the City of Sparta.

———————

To get to the City of Sparta, Wisconsin, take Interstate 90 exit #25 or #28.

To get to the trailhead parking in Sparta, take Interstate 90 exit #28. Proceed on Highway 16 west for 1.8 miles to East Avenue. Turn left on East Avenue for .1 mile to Walrath Street. Turn left on Walrath Street for .3 mile to John Street. Take a right on John Street (becomes Igloo Rd.) for 1.0 mile to Imac Avenue. Turn left on Imac Avenue into the trailhead parking area. For those who travel with a GPS, the coordinates of the Sparta Trailhead parking lot are N 43 55.600—W 90 47.300 with an elevation of 800 feet.

To get to the Sparta Depot, take Interstate 90 exit #28. Take Highway 16 west for 2.2 miles. Turn left at the stoplight on S. Water Street for .5 mile. Turn left on Milwaukee Street and the Sparta Depot is immediately on your right. For those who travel with a GPS, the coordinates of the Sparta Depot are N 43 55.909—W 90 48.592 with an elevation of 780 feet.

In case of emergencies the Sparta police and ambulance respond to 911.

Sparta Area Chamber of Commerce and Tourism Promotion Bureau, 111 Milwaukee Street, Sparta, WI 54656, 1-608-269-4123

Sparta Convention & Visitors Bureau, 123 N. Water Street, Sparta, WI 54656, 1-800-354-bike, www.spartawisconsin.org, bikeme@centurytel.net

Deke Slayton Memorial Space & Bike Museum, 200 W. Main Street, Sparta, WI 54656, 1-888-200-5302, www.spartan.org/dekeslaytonmu-seum, dekeslayton@centurytel.net

Country Inn, Corner of Interstate 90 and Highway 27 (exit #25), Sparta, WI 54656, 1-608-269-3110. To get to the Country Inn from the Sparta Depot, turn south .8 mile on S. Water Street. Curve right at the Y in the road. Water Street becomes Avon Rd. From the Y in the road, it is .8 mile to the Country Inn parking lot. For those of you who travel with a GPS, the coordinates of the Country Inn are N 43 55.355—W 90 49.165.

Slice of Chicago, 507 W. Wisconsin Street, Sparta, WI 54656, 1-608-269-2181. For those of you who travel with a GPS, the coordinates of Slice of Chicago are N 43 56.336—W 90 49.070.

Leon Valley Campground, 9050 Jancing Ave., Sparta, WI 54656, 1-608-269-6400

Heritage Motel, 704 W. Wisconsin Street, Sparta, WI 54656, 1-608-269-6991

Chapter 12

"400" State Trail

The "400" State Trail officially opened in June of 1993. This 22-mile trail lies on a rail line abandoned by the Chicago and NorthWestern Railroad that runs from the City of Elroy on the north end to the City of Reedsburg on the south. Along the way it passes through the Villages of Union Center, Wonewoc, and LaValle. This trail was named after the famous Mankato 400 diesel passenger train that is said to have been able to travel from Chicago, Illinois to Mankato, Minnesota in 400 minutes. The Mankato 400 traveled this rail line starting in 1942.

Covered in crushed limestone screenings, the "400" trail is easily traversed with any type of bicycle. On your ride you will witness wetlands, sandstone bluffs, rolling farmlands, pastures, and small towns. The trail parallels both the Baraboo River and Highway 33. Watch for many species of wildlife along the trail including sandhill cranes, beavers, badgers, deer, and wild turkeys. One unique feature of this trail is the 7 mile horse path that parallels the "400" trail between the Villages of Wonewoc and LaValle. It probably does not make much difference, but if you want to ride primarily downhill ride southbound.

Out of the Village of Elroy traveling southbound, you will cross the Baraboo River 3 times and tributaries of the Baraboo too many times to count. The wetlands and prairies visible along the path highlight this area.

Unfortunately, a 2-lane highway runs parallel and close to the bike trail so be prepared for vehicular noise.

In 4 miles you will encounter the Village of Union Center. With a population of 197 this area offers a motel, liquidation store, convenience store, and several bars and grills. From the Village of Union Center watch for the 4 mile extension to the trail that proceeds westbound to the Village of Hillsboro.

In another 3 miles of biking south from the Village of Union Center on the "400" trail, comes the Village of Wonewoc, a municipality of 830 people. Baker Field is a city park that is located on the "400" trail and offers a covered shelter, restrooms, lighted tennis court, and ball fields. The American Legion Park in Wonewoc offers a swimming pool and shower facility. A campground is also located at this park. A motel, laundromat, medical clinic, and five restaurants are available in Wonewoc.

As you ride southbound 7.2 miles on the "400" trail you will encounter the Village of LaValle (population 446) which bills itself as "the crossroads to the lakes" because it lies between Dutch Hollow and Lake Redstone, both man-made lakes. Here you will find a city park with restrooms, a large shelter, tennis and basketball courts, and baseball facilities. Services in LaValle include two restaurants, two bars, gas, groceries, hardware, laundromat, a B & B, and five churches.

In another 7.8 miles is the City of Reedsburg, which is a city of 5,834 people that offers the traveler most any service needs. The renovated depot in Reedsburg serves as the trail headquarters and offices for the Reedsburg Chamber of Commerce. Stop to see the interpretive displays and pick up free maps. Bicycles and child trailers are also available for rent at the depot. Reedsburg boasts it is within 30 miles of major attractions such as Wisconsin Dells, Circus World Museum, Devil's Lake State Park, MidContinent Railroad Museum, and the House on the Rock. If you enjoy old homes, Reedsburg offers many that are listed on the Federal Register of Historic Places. Most services that you would need including parks, shopping, restaurants, motels, B&B's, and a campground are but a small part that this great city has to offer.

~———~——~

To get to the City of Elroy, Wisconsin, take Interstate 90/94 to the Mauston exit # 69. Proceed on Highway 82 (Highway 82 makes many turns in Mauston) west 11 miles to Highway 80. Highway 82 west and Highway 80 south merge at this point.

To get to the Elroy Commons, take Highway 82 west and Highway 80 south (once they merge) for 1.2 miles to Cedar Street. Turn left on Cedar Street for .2 mile to a stop sign at Second Street (not marked). Turn right on Second Street and proceed for .1 mile. Turn right on Juneau Street, and take this street one block to the Elroy Commons. For those who travel with a GPS, the coordinates of the Elroy Commons are N 43 44.394—W 90 16.217 with an elevation of 997 feet.

In case of emergencies the Elroy Police and ambulance respond to 911.

To get to Reedsburg, Wisconsin, take Interstate 90/94 exit #89. Take Highway 23 west 8 miles to Highways 33/23 then west 6 miles to downtown Reedsburg. For those who travel with a GPS, the coordinates of the Reedsburg Depot trail headquarters are N 43.31.46—W 89.59.76 with an elevation of 901 feet.

In case of emergencies the Reedsburg Police and ambulance respond to 911.

"400" State Trail Headquarters, 240 Railroad Street, P.O. Box 142, Reedsburg, WI 53959, 1-608-524-2850

Chapter 13

Omaha Trail

The Omaha Trail is a delightful little trail that differs significantly from the others in this area. First, the Omaha Trail is not owned by the State as other trails are. It is owned by Juneau County and operated by the Juneau County Land, Forest, and Parks Department. Second, this trail is paved! No limestone screening getting the chain on your expensive bike dusty on this ride.

Opened in 1992 the Omaha Trail was built on the rail bed abandoned by the Chicago and NorthWestern Railroad. On this 13-mile trail you will see a mixture of farmland, sandstone cliffs, forests, and wet lands.

Traversing between the City of Elroy on the south and Village of Camp Douglas to the north, the Omaha trail passes through the Village of Hustler.

Moving north of the Elroy Commons area watch for the road signs that direct you toward the Omaha Trail. You will be riding on town roads and cross a recently constructed covered footbridge before leaving Elroy. At the edge of town please be careful as you cross the two-lane highway.

After a pleasant 6.5 miles of biking, you will encounter the only tunnel that Wisconsin has to offer on a bike trail besides the three on the Elroy Sparta Trail. This 875 foot long tunnel has a personality all its own. With rock sides and a man-made (steel) structure supporting the ceiling, this tunnel is wonderful to walk through. You will find a fantastic rest area with washroom, water, and a picnic table immediately north of the tunnel on the west side of the trail.

Billed as "the one and only in the world (until proven otherwise)" the Village of Hustler sits 2.5 miles north of the tunnel on the Omaha Trail. Keep your eyes open for the occasional deer or wild turkey that are sometimes seen along this section of the trail. Don't expect many services from Hustler! Three bars, a cheese factory, bank, convenience store, and 156 friendly people make up this village.

In 3.0 miles you will find the Village of Camp Douglas (population 512) which began in the mid 1800's as a logging camp due to its location where the Chicago and NorthWestern and the Soo Line Railroads crossed. Now it is best known for its two military installations. Camp Williams is an Army facility and Volk Field is affiliated with the Air National Guard. Visitors are welcome at Volk Field's impressive Wisconsin National Guard Museum, and I recommend the stop. Here you can view displays of military aircraft and other military artifacts. The Village of Camp Douglas offers its visitors restaurants, grocery stores, churches, a motel, laundromat, and several neighborhood bars. Public parking, washrooms, and water are available near the trailhead.

Most people that visit the area don't know about this little gem of a trail. Don't miss it.

———

To get to the City of Elroy, Wisconsin, take Interstate 90/94 to the Mauston exit # 69. Proceed on Highway 82 (Highway 82 makes many turns in Mauston) west 11 miles to Highway 80. Highway 82 west and Highway 80 south merge at this point.

To get to the Elroy Commons, take Highway 82 west and Highway 80 south (once they merge) for 1.2 miles to Cedar Street. Turn left on Cedar Street for .2 mile to a stop sign at Second Street (not marked). Turn right on Second Street and proceed for .1 mile. Turn right on Juneau Street, and take this street one block to the Elroy Commons. For those who travel with a GPS, the coordinates of the Elroy Commons are N 43 44.394—W 90 16.217 with an elevation of 997 feet.

In case of emergencies the Elroy police and ambulance respond to 911.

To get to the Village of Camp Douglas, Wisconsin, take Interstate 90/94 exit #55. At the bottom of the ramp, go toward the Village of Camp Douglas. Turn right and go .4 mile on Highways 12, 16, and C. Turn left on County H (County H will curve many times in town) for .5 mile to the trail. There is plenty of parking on the streets near the trail-head. For those who travel with a GPS, the coordinates of the Camp Douglas Trailhead are N 43 55.104—W 90 16.028 with an elevation of 975 feet.

In case of emergencies the Village of Camp Douglas area police and ambulance respond to 911.

You will experience a drop of 22 feet in elevation when biking north-bound on the Omaha Trail for an average of a 2% grade. When I last rode this trail southbound, I could feel the 13-mile non-stop uphill drag on my legs. I suggest northbound travel for a more enjoyable bike ride.

Chapter 14

La Crosse River State Trail

The La Crosse River State Trail is a very straight 21.5 mile trail that is built on the abandoned Chicago and North Western Railroad line between the City of Sparta and the Town of Medary. It parallels the La Crosse River and a very active rail line. At times you will be able to wave to the train engineers as freight and Amtrak trains roll past. Although you will see mostly farmland, you will also bike through prairie remnants, hardwood forests, and wetlands. The Villages of Rockland, Bangor, and West Salem lie along this trail. With a 115-foot change in elevation, biking west will afford you a slight downhill ride.

From the Sparta Depot, bike west for 6 miles to the Village of Rockland. A bedroom community of 509 residents, Rockland has a strong history. At one time this town hosted two banks, feed store, feed mill, two department stores, blacksmith shop, lumber yard, creamery, cheese factory, ice house, two stock yards, two railroad depots, hotel, restaurant, tavern, four grocery stores, cement block factory, post office, and saw mill. When European settlers came here in the 1840's, they called their town Fish Creek. However, they found that a village in Door County already used this name. So they named their town Rockland due to the castle-like sandstone rock just south of the trail in town by the mile marker 15 going east and 6 going west. Today, the tired bike rider will find only a bench and drinking water here.

Traveling west for another 3.5 miles you will come across the Village of Bangor and its 1076 residents. The first European settlers in this area were Welsh and named the town after their home in Wales. Swiss immigrants were the next to settle this area, with some descendants of these early settlers still living nearby. In this town you will find the home of a few businesses, schools, parks, and churches that serve the surrounding farming communities. Be careful when driving in Bangor since streets and parks are not marked well.

Five more miles of riding west will find you in the middle of the Village of West Salem, the home of 3,611 people. Nearby, the now defunct town of Neshonoc was where Hamlin Garlin, the Pulitzer Prize winning author, was born in 1860. In West Salem a visitor can view three homes listed on the Register of Historic Places, the "Octagon House," the "Old Salem House," and the "Garland Homestead."

Between the Villages of West Salem and Medary, is a short connecting trail (very well marked on the trail) to Veterans Memorial Campground. This is a full service campground. The short connecting trail is .5 mile long and goes under the railroad tracks through an interesting concrete structure. At the campground, you can purchase refreshments and use the washroom.

Medary marks the location where the La Crosse River Trail and Highway 16 meet. This area is located seven miles west of West Salem and you will find a golf course, parking area with washrooms, and some services.

If you are looking for services, La Crosse (very close to this trail) is truly a metropolitan city. Nestled at the confluence of the Mississippi, Black and La Crosse Rivers, this city is the home to 51,000 people. Everything a visitor could want can be found in La Crosse, from universities to breweries and everything in-between. With a port for three different riverboats, you can enjoy the river surroundings and view eagles on excursion trips up and down the Mississippi River.

Although Highway 16 officially ends the La Crosse River State Trail, I suggest you follow the bike trail another 2 miles over the foot bridge and along the connector trail so you can reach the information center for the Great River State Trail, where parking, rest rooms, and information is available.

———·——·——

To get to the Sparta Depot, take Interstate 90 exit #28. Take Highway 16 west for 2.2 miles. Turn left at the stoplight on S. Water Street for .5 mile. Turn left on Milwaukee Street and the Sparta Depot is immediately on your right. For those who travel with a GPS, the coordinates of the Sparta Depot are N 43 55.909—W 90 48.592 with an elevation of 780 feet.

In case of emergencies the Sparta police and ambulance respond to 911.

To get to the Medary Trailhead parking area, take Interstate 90 exit #4. Proceed .7 mile on Highway 157 east. Turn right on Highway 16 west for .6 mile. Turn left on County B for .4 mile. The trailhead parking in on your left. For those who travel with a GPS, the coordinates of the trailhead parking area are N 43 51.576—W 90 12.119 with an elevation of 665 feet.

To get to Onalaska, Wisconsin and the Great River State Trail Information Center (Onalaska Center for Commerce and Tourism), take Interstate 90 exit #3. Proceed north on Highway 35 for .6 mile. Turn right on Oak Forest Drive, and the parking is immediately on your right. For those who travel with a GPS, the coordinates of the Information Center are N 43 52.489—W 90 13.738 with an elevation of 671 feet.

In case of emergencies in this area dial 911.

You will experience a drop of 115 feet in elevation when biking westbound on the La Crosse River State Trail. If you are interested in taking the slightly downhill route, I suggest you bike westbound.

La Crosse Convention and Visitors Bureau, Riverside Park, P.O. Box1895, La Crosse, WI 54602-1895, 1-608-782-2366

Chapter 15

Great River State Trail

The Great River State Trail was established in 1967. It follows an abandoned Chicago and NorthWestern Railroad line between Onalaska, Wisconsin on the south and Marshland, Wisconsin on the north passing through Midway, Lytles Landing, and Trempealeau.

While riding this trail you will see majestic limestone bluffs, wetlands, lakes, and the banks of the Mississippi River. Eighteen bridges cross the many rivers, streams, and wetlands along its 22.5 mile length. Just some of the watersheds that you cross on the Great River State Trail are the Black River, Shingle Creek, Tanks Creek, and Halfway Creek all draining into the nearby Mississippi River.

Many species of wildlife can be seen here, but birds are the most spectacular. Watch for ducks, great blue herons, egrets, and the occasional bald eagle.

Onalaska is a charming suburb of La Crosse. Overlooking the Mississippi River, this town has everything that a visitor to the Great River State Trail needs. Motels, restaurants, groceries, gasoline, and bicycle repair are available here. Parking at the trailhead includes washrooms and a small concession.

Bicycle north following the Great River State Trail 14 miles to the town of Trempealeau (population 1,039). This amazing little town is a definite place to stop and enjoy the day. Trempealeau meaning "mountain soaking in the water" is the home of Perrot State Park, which features a great family camping area, hiking trails, and ball fields. The town of Trempealeau features the historic Trempealeau Hotel. This wonderful hotel features lunch and dinner with views of the Mississippi River from the dinning room, screened porch, sun deck, or beer garden.

Along the Mississippi River you can observe barges negotiating Lock and Dam #6. These huge containers carry mostly grain, wood, and coal.

North 8.5 miles will be Marshland and the end of the trail where a parking area awaits your arrival.

To get to Onalaska, Wisconsin and the Great River State Trail Information Center (Onalaska Center for Commerce and Tourism), take Interstate 90 exit #3. Proceed north on Highway 35 for .6 mile. Turn right on Oak Forest Drive, and the parking is immediately on your right. For those who travel with a GPS, the coordinates of the Information Center are N 43 52.489—W 90 13.738 with an elevation of 671 feet.

In case of emergencies dial 911.

To get to Marshland, Wisconsin at the northern end of the trail, take Interstate 90 exit #4. Drive north on Highway 53 for 18 miles to Highways 54/93, turn west 5 miles to Highways 35/54 drive west 6 miles to the Marshland Parking area. For those who travel with a GPS, the coordinates of Marshland, Wisconsin are N 43.04.29—W 90.33.31 with an elevation of 685 feet.

You will experience a gain of 14 feet in elevation when biking northbound so it does not make a difference which way you travel.

Onalaska Center for Commerce and Tourism, 800 Oak Forest Drive, Onalaska, WI 54650, 1-608-9570 & 1-800-873-1901

Perrot State Park, R. 1, Box 407, Trempealeau, WI 54661, 1-608-534-6409

The Historic Trempealeau Hotel, 150 Main Street, Trempealeau, WI 54661, 1-608-534-6898

Chapter 16

A Great Family Vacation

Are you looking for a great family getaway without spending too much money? The Elroy Sparta Bicycle Trail can be the basis for trips ranging from a weekend to two weeks. This area of Wisconsin has a lot to offer a family, and it is readily accessible by car in less than a days drive by families living in and around most major cities in Wisconsin, Minnesota, Iowa, Illinois, and much of Michigan. I believe this is a great family vacation area. I began vacationing here with my family when the children were still babies in the mid 1980's, and the Elroy Sparta Trail is still a vacation requested by my children every year.

For the family that enjoys camping, I suggest that you stay at Tunnel Trail Campground. This family run campground offers most everything you could want. Sites range from tent only grassy plots, a camping cabin, to fully improved pull through sites. The heated swimming pool offers a safe environment to relax after a good day on the bike and a place where the children can go when mom and dad are worn out. Children will find the game room entertaining while adults will find a very unique reading room chock full of old paperbacks. Probably best of all, the Tunnel Trail Campground is literally located on the trail. In fact you will cross the trail while driving from the local road into the campground. From your campsite your children never have to cross or come close to a road to bike on the trail. You can feel safe just letting them ride to Tunnel #1 on their own.

I suggest you make your reservations early because this marvelous place fills every weekend during the biking season.

For those who prefer hotel accommodations I suggest you stay at the Country Inn in Sparta. The rooms are just fine, though some might find them slightly small, and the price is right. Conveniently located near the bike trail, this is the perfect home base. The Inn's advantage over other lodging in the area is the indoor pool and spa and its continental breakfast.

In the town of Ontario you will find one of the great canoe rivers in the area. The Kickapoo River is easily floatable by families. I would always suggest some instruction before canoeing, but this river is not difficult to navigate. Titanic Canoe Rentals will set you up with the boats, paddles, and personal floatation devices that you will need. They put you in the river at their property and will pick your party up at most any point you ask. Tell them how long you want to float and they will be there waiting for you when you are done.

For families who need an amusement park atmosphere, the Wisconsin Dells is about an hour drive. You can find go-carts, thrill rides, water parks, horseback rides, restaurants, and hundreds of holes of mini golf. The famous Wisconsin Ducks are amphibious vehicles that travel through the woods and on the Wisconsin River giving the family the best view of the river and a fun time. The Tommy Bartlett Thrill Show is water skiing tricks and clowns galore. Be aware, I am not the only Dad to have spent more money per day in the Wisconsin Dells than at Walt Disney World.

Near the Dells is the town of Baraboo, Wisconsin. Here you will find the International Crane Foundation where a family can visit possibly the world's most renowned facility dedicated to the study and preservation of the Sandhill Crane, one of the most beautiful birds of North America. The Circus World Museum in Baraboo provides the family with a look into the past and a glimpse of the future of the Circus industry. A historical tour of Circus artifacts, a working big top, and clown make-up artists showing their craft are just a few of the surprises you will see here. Plan at least half a day for this visit. In Baraboo, Devil's Lake State Park provides camping, swimming, rock climbing, canoeing, and recreational fields.

In nearby North Freedom, Wisconsin the MidContinent Railroad Museum is a must see. Here you can take a memorable, 50-minute round trip ride on steam engine train with restored coaches built in 1915. Call for departure times.

If you enjoy military displays, a trip to the Village of Camp Douglas to visit the Wisconsin National Guard Memorial Library and Museum is worth your time. Don't expect this to be a full day event, but I would set aside two hours to tour this fine facility.

A trip into the City of Sparta is a must. The Deke Slayton Memorial Space & Bike Museum may sound like a very strange combination, but it works better than it sounds. Astronaut Deke Slayton was raised nearby, and the section of the museum dedicated to him chronicles the early NASA space program highlighting the Apollo missions and the Space Shuttle. Many artifacts from space travel are displayed along with personal items donated by Mr. Slayton. The bicycle section of this museum has more than 30 antique bikes on display. Teaching children about the history of the pedal powered vehicle they now ride on the trail and the impact of the bicycle on the formation of our society is both educational and fun. Plus, if they begin to complain when another child passes them on the bike trail with a cooler bike, you can remind them of the wooden wheeled, one speed bike with no seat that you saw in the museum. Make sure that you enjoy dinner at Len and Barb's Slice of Chicago while in town.

Chapter 17

The Perfect Trip for Two

Looking for a getaway? You will find the Elroy Sparta Trail is just what is needed to work out the kinks. The best time to visit would be during the week, but a weekend getaway can still be enjoyed if you book the rooms in advance.

Stay at the Country Inn in Sparta. The rooms are just fine, though some might find them slightly small, and the price is right. Conveniently located near the bike trail, this is the perfect home base. The Inn's advantage over other lodging in the area is the indoor pool and spa and its continental breakfast.

Arranged in advance, a pick-up in the morning by Out Spokin' Adventures is great. This service will pick you up at the hotel in their 15 passenger vans, put your bike on a rack on the roof and drive you to any place you want on the trail. With this service, you only have to ride one direction on the trail. During the drive to your put-in, the people from Out Spokin' will fill you in on the trail's history, the best places to eat, and the charm of the surrounding area. This is the best service on the trail.

After a long bike ride and a longer time in the hot tub at the hotel, it's time for dinner. Only a fool would miss Len and Barb's Slice of Chicago. My favorite is the Lasagna while my wife enjoys the Sparta Turnover. After dinner the Star Cinema is a six-screen theater showing the latest movies. The perfect nightcap in my book is a stop at the Dairy Queen before bed.

Chapter 18

Bob's Favorites

Breakfast:	Dorset Valley School Restaurant & Bakery
	(800) 775-0698
Lunch:	Gina's Pies Are Square
	400 Main Street
	Wilton, WI 54670
	1-608-435-6541
Dinner:	Slice of Chicago
	507 W. Wisconsin Street
	Sparta, WI 54656
	1-608-269-2181
Snack:	A & W Drive-In
	Wisconsin Street & S Water Street
	Sparta, WI 54656
B&B:	Trail-Side Bed & Breakfast
	(800) 775-0698
Campground:	Tunnel Trail Campground
	Route 1 Box 185
	Wilton, WI 54670
	Tunneltrail@elroynet.com
	(608) 435-6829 (in season) & (920) 294-3742
	(off-season)

Hotel:	Country Inn
	Corner of Interstate 90 and Highway 27
	Sparta, WI 54656
	1-608-269-3110
Canoe Rental:	Titanic Canoe Rental
	Highway 131 & Main Street
	Ontario, WI 54651
	1-608-337-4551 & 1-877-get-sunk
	www.titaniccanoerental.com
	jasonteynot@hotmail.com
Shuttle Service:	Out Spokin' Adventures
	409 N. Court Street
	Sparta, WI 54656
	1-800-4we-bike
	www.outspokinadventures.com
	outspokin@centurytel.net
Map:	American Bike Trails
	1430 Main Street
	Suite 525
	Des Plaines, IL 60016
Bike Repair:	Speed's Bicycle Shop
	1126 John Street
	Sparta, WI 54656
	1-608-269-2315
Direction to Bike:	Westbound on the Elroy Sparta Trail

Conclusion

I hope this book will be useful to you in your travels to the section on earth that I love the most. Don't forget to periodically check this book's companion website at www.ElroySparta.com for periodic updates.

I hope to see you on the trail.

About the Author

Bob Sobie is an avid recreational bicycle rider. He especially enjoys riding the many spectacular rails-to-trails that are available in the United States. Among his favorite trails are the Elroy Sparta Trail, "400," Omaha, La Crosse River, Great River, Military Ridge, Sugar River, and the Glacial Drumlin Trail in Wisconsin; the Illinois Prairie Path, Great Western, Fox River, Chicago Lakefront, and Illinois-Michigan Canal in Illinois; and the Katy Trail in Missouri.

Bob resides with his family in Glen Ellyn, Illinois. He is a professor at the College of DuPage in Glen Ellyn, where he teaches Automotive Service Technology, Speech Communications, and Field Studies. In his role as an instructor in the Field Studies Department, Bob has taken groups of students many times to the Elroy Sparta Trail to help students enjoy his passion for this delightful trail. Bob holds a Masters of Arts in Communication, a Masters of Science in Education, a Bachelors of Science in Education, and an Associate of Applied Science Degree. To contact the author, please e-mail him at ElroySparta@aol.com.

Bob Sobie

References

"400" State Trail Headquarters
240 Railroad Street
P.O. Box 142
Reedsburg, WI 53959
1-608-524-2850

American Bike Trails
1430 Main Street
Suite 525
Des Plaines, IL 60016

Bike Trails Magazine
Foxxy Publications
P.O. Box 526
Sparta, WI 54656
1-608 269-5054

City of Elroy, Wisconsin
www.elroywi.com
elroywi@mwt.net.

Country Favorites
138 Main Street
Elroy, WI 53929
1-608-462-5468
favorites@elroynet.com

Country Inn
Corner of Interstate 90 and Highway 27
Sparta, WI 54656
1-608-269-3110

Country Livin' Motel
Highway 71
Kendall, WI 54638
1-608-463-7135 & 1-608-463-7329

Deke Slayton Memorial Space & Bike Museum
200 W. Main Street
Sparta, WI 54656
1-888-200-5302
www.spartan.org/dekeslaytonmuseum
dekeslayton@centurytel.net.

Diamond Lil's
201 Main Street
Norwalk, WI 54648
1-608-823-7708

Dorset Valley School Restaurant & Bakery
26147 State Highway 71
Wilton, WI 54670
1-800-775-0698

Elroy Area Advancement Corporation
P.O. Box 52
Elroy, WI 53929
1-800-606-bike

Gina's Pies Are Square
400 Main Street
Wilton, WI 54670
1-608-435-6541

Heritage Motel
704 W. Wisconsin Street
Sparta, WI 54656
1-608-269-6991

Hidden Valleys of Southwestern Wisconsin
Hidden Valleys, Inc.
P.O. Box 29
Richland Center, WI 53581
1-608-647-2243

Jim's Trailside Deli & Ice Cream Parlor
302 Railroad Street
Elroy, WI 53929
1-608-462-2212

Judy's Trailside Café
Mill Street & the trail
Norwalk, WI 54648

Kendall Food Center
Highway 71
Kendall, WI 54638
1-608-463-3663

La Crosse Convention and Visitors Bureau
Riverside Park, P.O. Box 1895
La Crosse, WI 54602-1895
1-608-782-2366

Leon Valley Campground
9050 Jancing Ave.
Sparta, WI 54656
1-608-269-6400

Midway Restaurant & Bar
Highway 71
Kendall, WI 54638
1-608-463-7170

Monroe County Visitor
June 2000-May 2001

Nelson's NAPA Auto Service
1410 Academy Street
Elroy, WI 53929
1-608-462-5138

Norwalk Village Office
P.O. Box 51
Norwalk , WI 54648
1-608-823-7760
www.windingrivers.com/norwalk.html
villageofnorwalk@centuryinter.net.

Onalaska Center for Commerce and Tourism
800 Oak Forest Drive
Onalaska, WI 54650
1-608-9570 & 1-800-873-1901

Out Spokin' Adventures
409 N. Court Street
Sparta, WI 54656
1-800-4we-bike
www.outspokinadventures.com
outspokin@centurytel.net

Perrot State Park
R. 1, Box 407
Trempealeau, WI 54661
1-608-534-6409

Slice of Chicago
507 W. Wisconsin Street
Sparta, WI 54656
1-608-269-2181

Sparta Area Chamber of Commerce and Tourism Promotion Bureau
111 Milwaukee Street
Sparta, WI 54656
1-608-269-4123

Sparta Convention & Visitors Bureau
123 N. Water Street
Sparta, WI 54656
1-800-354-bike
www.spartawisconsin.org
bikeme@centurytel.net.

The Historic Trempealeau Hotel
150 Main Street
Trempealeau, WI 54661
1-608-534-6898

Titanic Canoe Rental
Highway 131 & Main Street
Ontario, WI 54651
1-608-337-4551 & 1-877-get-sunk
www.titaniccanoerental.com
jasonteynot@hotmail.com

Trail-Side Bed & Breakfast
1-800-775-0698

Tunnel Trail Campground
Route 1 Box 185
Wilton, WI 54670
Tunneltrail@elroynet.com
1-608-435-6829 (in season)
1-920-294-3742 (off-season)

Wildcat Mountain State Park
Ontario, WI
1-608-337-4775

Wilton Fastrip
Highway 71
Wilton, WI 54670
1-608-435-6977

Wilton Village Park information
1-608-435-6666
www.windingrivers.com/wilton.html

Winding Rivers Review
The Kickapoo Valley Press
P.O. Box 7
Ontario, WI 54651
1-608-337-4232

Bibliography

Anderson, Leonard R. *History of Chicago and NorthWestern Railroad Line–Elroy to Sparta Now Elroy-Sparta Trail*. October 1968.

Bike Trails Magazine. Sparta, Wisconsin: Foxxy Publications, 2000.

Elroy Sparta State Trail Map WI-01, American Bike Trails.

Hidden Valleys of Southwestern Wisconsin. Richland Center, WI: Hidden Valleys, Inc., 2000.

History of the Elroy Sparta Trail.

Jaffe, Harry. "Pride & Joy in Illinois." *Rails to Trails*. Winter 2001: 8-12.

Monroe County Visitor. June 2000-May 2001.

The Blend of Yesterday and Today on the Elroy Sparta Trail.

Winding Rivers Review. Ontario, WI: Kickapoo Valley Press, 2000.

Index

Trail Maps

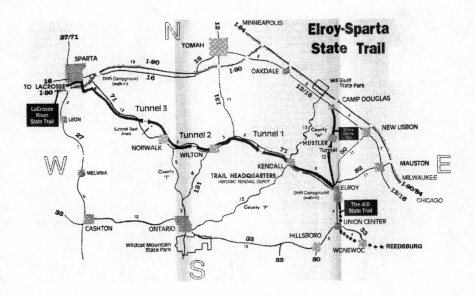

Elroy Sparta Trail Map

"400 State Trail Map

OMAHA TRAIL

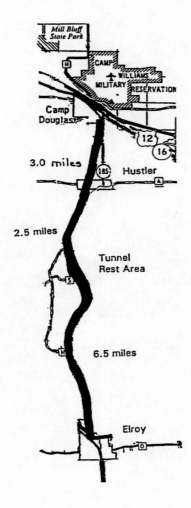

Omaha Trail Map

La Crosse River State Trail Map

Great River State Trail Map